Beyond Day Ten

Practical Advice on
Establishing a Vipassana Practice

I0159840

Corinne Bilyayev

Vipassana Research Publications

Vipassana Research Publications
an imprint of
Pariyatti Publishing
www.pariyatti.org

First Pariyatti Edition 2025

ISBN: 978-1-68172-852-0 (paperback)
ISBN: 978-1-68172-853-7 (ePub)
ISBN: 978-1-68172-854-4 (Mobi)
ISBN: 978-1-68172-855-1 (PDF)

Table of Contents

1. Introduction   1

2. Goenkaji's Recommendation for
   Daily Practice   3

3. Seeing Benefits and Noticing Progress   5

4. Real Talk about Hindrances and
   Other Challenges   7

5. Sīla   21

6. Pāramī   29

7. The Importance of Friendship   43

8. Pariyatti   45

9. Group Sits   47

10. Service   49

11. Sitting Once a Year   51

12. Conclusion   53

Acknowledgements   55

1

Introduction

The aim of this book is to help energize your practice of Vipassana and inspire you to continue on the Path even while outside of a vipassana center. It is written for Old Students who have completed at least one ten-day course under S.N. Goenka's assistant teachers and are serious about wanting to continue practicing at home. I've not made any attempt to clarify Pāli terms used during the courses. (If you are not an Old Student but happened upon this book and would like to know more about the courses, please go to dhamma.org)

I started writing this book after several weekends of giving part-time service at my closest Vipassana center. During the late summer months, there happened to be a chronic shortage of servers, so I decided to go as often as possible even though I couldn't stay ten days at a time. This allowed me to serve with a large number of Old Students and make several new friends on the Path. During many conversations in the Dhamma kitchen, one theme often surfaced: daily practice.

I found that many of the servers were not successfully maintaining a daily practice, despite their enormous efforts in completing courses, genuinely intending to practice, and even serving courses. People were hungry to know how I've kept it up. So, in this book, I will share the experience of maintaining my own practice by reviewing the Dhamma I ground my practice in and explaining the practical application of it with examples from my life. There is no discussion of the technique itself nor any claim to any kind of authoritative knowledge whatsoever. I am merely a fellow Old Student, and this book is my best effort to include you in the ongoing Dhamma kitchen conversation about how to make daily practice a reality.

2

Goenkaji's Recommendation for Daily Practice

During the Day 11 closing discourse, Goenka, or Goenkaji as some respectfully call him, instructs us to practice at least one hour in the morning and one hour in the evening. For the purposes of having a common practice goal for readers of this book, we will aim for any one hour in the morning and any one hour in the evening, with the understanding that more or less strictness with that routine is possible. We should also aim to be mindful that these meditation sessions are not to create a rite—nor are they just boxes to check on a to-do list, but are genuine practice times during which we must make a sincere effort to practice the technique we learned during our course with Goenkaji.

3

Seeing Benefits and Noticing Progress

The specific benefits you get from practice will depend on many factors, but in general, you should see some kind of improvements in your life. Goenkaji tells us the practice brings fruits here and now as well as down the road. Personally, I've seen too many practical benefits to even list, but I will highlight some major ones. The point of this list is to show that maintaining daily practice is valuable, not only in a spiritual sense like increasing our *pāramī*, or good qualities, but also in mundane ways.

- Better relations with my children
- Better relations with my partner
- Increased patience with difficult life circumstances
- Increased tolerance of separation from loved ones
- Better physical health

- Better communication
- Better diet

Progress on the path is measured by our increased equanimity. And the more equanimous we become, the more our minds get "...filled up with loving-kindness, compassion, and sympathetic joy. When this happens, the student starts creating an environment of peace and happiness for oneself as well as for others." as Goenkaji writes in the article called "Progress in Vipassana Meditation."

4

Real Talk about
Hindrances and Other Challenges

On Day 6, Goenkaji warns us about five hindrances or enemies to meditation, the five *nīvaraṇa*. They are craving, aversion, drowsiness, agitation, and doubt. Additionally, Sayagyi U Ba Khin identifies ten soldiers of Mara whom he defines as the "personification of negative forces". They are the "desire to enjoy sense pleasures..., unwillingness to reside or be happy in a quiet place..., hunger..., craving for various tastes and foods..., drowsiness..., being afraid of solitude..., doubt..., becoming proud and arrogant when the meditation is successful...", and the last two concerning teachers: becoming conceited, and creating false Dhamma to please students and receive "homage and offerings."

Even though we can all indentify with those challenges and hindrances emphasized by our teachers, I want to give certain challenges some extra attention based on conversations I've had with other Old Students who are struggling to practice.

1. Sleep

Goenkaji says in the Day 11 discourse that part of the time you need for meditation will be gained from a reduced need for sleep. Although increased meditation can mean the need for less sleep, if you decide to meditate by robbing yourself of sleep, you might be setting yourself up for exhaustion. I remind myself not to set expectations that if I meditate for two hours, I'll suddenly be able to function well with two hours less sleep. There are plenty of daily activities to subtract minutes from to help find time to meditate, not only sleep. Shorter showers, less television, less time online, simpler meals, less idle talk, less time pursuing fruitless hobbies, etc., all yield more opportunity to meditate. Creating new habits takes repetition and effort, and this practice is no different.

In general, meditating makes me more focused on how I spend my time, which, for me at least, translates as less wasted time in bed, but not necessarily less actual sleep at this point. However, how I define sleep has also changed over the course of my practice. Before meditation, sleep meant deep sleep to me—a complete lack of awareness of my surroundings, possibly some drooling! Now my definition of sleep also includes what I might have considered being only half-asleep in the past. So, by those definitions, my amount of sleep has definitely decreased, and my hours of awareness, though partial and inconsistent, are increasing even outside of formal meditation.

2. Sex

Let's be honest. If you're in a relationship, the last thing you do together in the evening or the first thing in the morning probably isn't meditation. It doesn't take long to figure out that meditation and sex are competing for the same periods of time. At this point, it becomes a matter of priority and determination. In my relationship, we are both committed to meditating now, but in the beginning, I hadn't been to a course yet. Often, I would wake up to find my partner sitting in the corner of the room meditating. There were days when I felt slighted or ignored, but even then, I knew on some level that my agitation was part of why I needed to meditate too.

At the beginning of our daily practice together, we were not careful about where we meditated vs. where we made love, and I felt it created a tangle of vibrations that was unhelpful. Over time we grew wiser about separating the spaces, and it became easier to practice because it was obvious which space we were in (see the upcoming section on meditation spaces).

Our routine has become meditation first in the morning, meditation last in the evening. The priority is to start and end the day in meditation. After all, we practice because we are seeking change. We each have to be personally willing to make it.

3. Children

In my experience, the other major in-house competition for meditation time comes from children. Five of our children live with us so you can imagine the endless permutations of "emergencies" they justify to interrupt meditation. In the beginning, it was a learning curve for all of us. I was determined not to let them keep me from establishing a new routine, and they were determined to test my determination! One of the most difficult days for me was when my then seven-year-old opened the door where I was sitting and said my name incessantly and unwrapped my meditation blanket from around my body. I persisted motionless and in silence, and eventually, she got bored and left. Of course, there are times when I do get up on account of the children, like if one of them is sick, for example, but generally, they've stopped interrupting just looking for attention.

Beyond attention-seeking, another reason they were interrupting—and I'm mentioning it because it had never occurred to me—was because they were simply very curious about what was going on behind the closed door for an hour. Evidently, meditation has had a lot of play in the media in various ways, and they wanted to know exactly what was happening. They would open the door to peek at random times and later explained they wanted to see if we were "levitating yet or still just sitting there!" So, I think it's worth this short paragraph to remind you of the benefits of teaching *ānāpāna* meditation to your children, so they have a clear picture of what you're doing! There is a widely available ten-minute mini-*ānāpāna* session online you can play for them called Mini Anapana for All.

Of course, beyond simply understanding what you're doing, teaching children *ānāpāna* gives them a chance to focus their own mind and gives them a way to participate if they choose to. To date, two of our children have participated in a children's course, and another has practiced alone. They all have a much deeper understanding and respect for the value and difficulty of the practice. This section is about children being a potential obstacle to our practice, but it would be wrong not to take the opportunity to mention the benefits of meditation for children. Suffice it to say, if your children learn *ānāpāna,* it will benefit your practice and plant the seed for their own.

Some strategies to meditate with children nearby:

- Post your end time on a closed door: "I'll be out at 8:10."
- Schedule your sit when they are less likely to

need you—while they are showering and getting ready for bed, for example.

- Give them tasks to complete during the hour—homework, folding laundry, etc.
- Set a time that you will be available for them: "I will sit now, but if you think of something you want to tell me, write it down and slide it under my door and I'll come to talk to you at 8:30."
- Give them headphones if they want to watch or listen to something that would bother you.
- Give yourself headphones if you want to listen to chanting without bothering them.
- Remind them that meditation makes you less reactive and a better parent, enlist their support.
- Teach them *ānāpāna*, take them to a children's course so they understand better what you're doing and can begin to meditate themselves.

4. Frustration

A common post-course feeling for me, and for others I've talked to, is that I quickly lose (so to speak) what I gained at the course, such as deep concentration, or the ability to sit still for longer periods, or deeper insights. There's a feeling that the 'something special' that can happen at a center won't happen at home. One time my partner asked me how my morning sit was, and I answered, "nothing special." Laughter ensued because of the reference to Goenkaji's Day 4 discourse, where he talks about his friend who was craving for something special and ignoring the reality of the moment. The friend had missed the entire purpose of the course.

While this frustration can happen anywhere, it's more likely to crop up while practicing at home. I forget that the practice is accepting what is. I'm still craving. I sign up for a course with some kind of expectation that it will be beneficial. When I decide to continue practicing at home, I have the same expectation. I want some kind of tangible benefit, and while the practice overall is enormously beneficial, sitting for an hour often doesn't necessarily yield any immediately noticeable gain. In addition, meditating at home, we don't have all the structural support of a course—no one is making meals for us, no one outside is maintaining silence, our days can be demanding and chaotic and stressful. It's easy to find excuses to fail. It's too noisy, I'm too tired, I'm just sitting here, and nothing is happening.

Another point about the frustrating feeling when you struggle to focus during your meditation and think you're doing "nothing" is that doing nothing is arguably much, much better than anything else you might do during that hour. When you sit to meditate but fall asleep or get lost in thought and lose track of breath or sensation, at least you're not committing any unwholesome actions. You might be rolling in thoughts, but you are still cultivating the right intention to meditate, and you are making the right effort by sitting there trying. And if you have even one moment of awareness during the hour, you've gained that much more than if you'd made no effort.

This insight is exactly the point I found I've missed when I feel frustrated with my practice—it's in the acceptance of our current miserable conditions that we learn equanimity. It's in noticing our ignorant frustration that we can become more deeply aware of our craving. It's in the "nothing" happening that everything we need to observe is happening.

The slight self-awareness I've developed of my ignorant frustration about how meditating at home feels compared to sitting a course has increased my determination to practice. My mindset now is, "I'm just going to sit here and try no matter what." And, really, that's all you have to do. I could (and sometimes do) beat myself up over the quality of my home practice and the general condition of my mind, but that's not helpful. The truth of the matter is my mind is very weak, meditation requires a lot of strength, and the only way to get from weakness to strength is to keep making an effort.

I'll talk more about the importance of annual courses in a later section, but daily practice is where much benefit is won, though this is perhaps harder to see because it can manifest so slowly. During a course, you might meditate ten hours a day, or approximately 100 hours. Practicing for a year at home for an hour in the morning and an hour in the evening, you will meditate approximately 730 hours! I don't want to underestimate the importance of that ongoing, long-term training.

In a question and answer from William Hart's *The Art of Living*, Goenkaji explains how we are to practice:

Answer: ...keep on observing the reality of this moment, and let enlightenment come. If it does not come, don't be upset. You just do your job and leave the result to Dhamma. If you work in this way, you are not attached to enlightenment, and it will certainly come... It is your responsibility to cleanse your own mind. Take it as a responsibility but do it without attachment.

Question: It's not to achieve anything?

Answer: No. Whatever comes will come by itself. Let it happen naturally.

5. Boredom

What am I doing just sitting here when there's so much else I could be doing?! When meditation is new, it feels exciting, like the smell of a new car. Every time we get into a new car, we are excited and sometimes feel like going for a drive just for the experience of it. But once we start daily commuting, running errands, bringing children here and there, the newness wears off and we don't feel excited anymore. Home practice can feel the same way, and when it does, it means we've missed the point. The vehicle's main purpose isn't for pleasure; it's for transportation. Meditation's main purpose isn't entertainment, though it might be a new "activity" for some of us, it's gaining mastery over our minds and attaining liberation. If boredom and restlessness set in, it's a clue my mind is craving something other than what I'm doing. At these times, I ask myself, why am I practicing? And my answer, to come out of the otherwise endless suffering, which I experience plenty of daily, is always sufficient to refocus me.

6. Food

Food can help or hinder our practice because it is a fuel source in our bodies that we perhaps don't need in the same way we once did. Through our ignorance, though, we often choose our food based on old habits, not necessity. For example, a pregnant woman needs extra calories, but she would suffer for that if she were to continue eating those extra calories indefinitely. As a meditator who practices daily, I find my mind is much less agitated than it used to be. I can no longer feed myself the way I used to.

In the past, when I was a meat-eater who didn't meditate, I tried being vegetarian and failed. Because my mind was full of impurities like anger and greed and passion, it couldn't support its constant level of agitation without the fleshy fuel of meat, and I felt I was starving. Physically, I had plenty of calories, but it didn't matter to my agitation. It wanted meat to support it. Now, because I've managed to remove some of the grosser impurities of my mind through the practice, I am quite happily vegetarian.

My diet is usually best right after a course. My body and mind feel very clean and light, and I find I eat much less on a course than usual, not just because no dinner is offered, but because I really wouldn't need dinner even if it were offered. But what happens on day 10 when I start talking again? Time to eat! Which leads me back to the important observation that often when I eat, I'm not feeding my body, I'm feeding my agitated mind. My body, as evidenced by eating less and feeling well during courses, needs very little food. But when I feel anger or sadness, or spend the day talking, etc. I seek much more food. Not because of any increase in physical exertion, simply an increase in unwholesome mental action sends me to the pantry to refuel.

So, there's a relationship between food and agitation that I can use to my advantage in practice. If I want a calmer mind, I can influence it by the type and quantity of food I take. And if I overeat, I immediately feel heavy and lethargic, and it's harder to concentrate. I marvel that I used to "need" that energy to fuel my hot, agitated mind and am grateful to note some progress.

Sometimes, depending on life circumstances, social eating and drinking can bring trouble if you're trying to maintain a new habit of eating consciously and abstaining from taking intoxicants. I've found a very simple answer, "No, thank you, I feel better when I don't eat/drink that" is enough to satisfy people. Most people know on some level that they would also feel better if they abstained from overeating and drinking, and there's no opportunity to argue because my answer is based on my bodily feeling and not on a judgment of their behavior.

7. Work

When I decided to sit a course for the first time, I was working a job paid on an hourly basis with varying hours, including sometimes overnight. I often had only eight hours between the end of one shift and the start of the next, which meant I had to travel home, eat, sleep, shower, and travel back to work all within those few hours. I also had to schedule my course four months ahead of time to have the necessary twelve days off approved by my boss. Luckily, by the time I went to sit, I had left that job for one with a much more forgiving schedule. When I returned after sitting the course, I had the time available I needed to start practicing.

You might say that was all a lucky coincidence, but I don't feel that way. I have observed time and time again that "Dhamma works", as Goenkaji says. When we are ready for something, the opportunity arises for us. I was ready to sit the course and ready to start practicing, and my new job made that possible. I believe that if you are alert to what's going on around you and are ready to commit to your practice, you will find that a way to make it happen will open up for you. That said, you may have to make sacrifices in order to take advantage of that opportunity—letting go is part of the practice, after all.

8. Space

When I first began practicing meditation at home, my partner and I sat in our bedroom together. In a previous section about 'Sex', I mentioned that wasn't the best idea! A daily conversation of which might happen first, sex or meditation, wasn't helping our practice or our relationship. Fairly soon, we moved our meditation mats to a separate space (which happened to be a large tent because the house didn't have extra space). The tent became our piece of Dhamma land, our sacred space. It helped the vibrations increase because nothing was disturbing the space during the day, no one else entered, and it was completely separate from the rest of the house. I've talked to other students who maintain a special space for only meditation, and they claim to feel benefits as well.

In general, if you can create a sacred space for your practice, however small or temporary, it's a positive step. The guidelines for home group-sit hosts are good guidelines for setting up your own meditation space: an area with no religious signs or symbols, no intoxicants, and no sexual activity. I find I also prefer an enclosed space rather than an open area like a living room.

That said, there are always numerous occasions to be flexible and times when you will have to sit in less-than-ideal places. During the course of my practice, I've often found myself away from home and away from my preferred meditation space. A common complaint I've heard from other students is that heavy travel schedules are a problem. I agree travel schedules can cause difficulties in practice, and conditions for meditating are often less than ideal, but certainly, it can all be figured out. After all, the most important (dare I say *only?*) variable in succeeding in meditation is the mindset, not location. I've sat in a friend's New York City living room at 2 AM, on full transatlantic flights, in airports, in the corner of shared hotel rooms, on trains, in the car between meetings, in a storage shed. All of those conditions sound very pleasant compared to the conditions we read monks describing. So, my point is, while the conditions we face may be difficult for us, we can admit they are not too difficult when we put them in perspective, and certainly not so difficult they can't be overcome by increased physical and mental effort.

5

Sīla

Goenkaji explains during the course that *sīla*, moral conduct, is the foundation we need to be able to concentrate our minds. The following are the precepts we agree to observe:

1. To abstain from killing any being;
2. To abstain from stealing;
3. To abstain from sexual misconduct (and during a course to abstain from all sexual activity);
4. To abstain from telling lies;
5. To abstain from all intoxicants.

During a course, we observe *sīla* because we want to participate in the course, and those are the rules of engagement, but afterward, we are free to do what we like. The question relevant to this book is, what effect does observing *sīla* have on my ability to practice at home?

In order to practice, I need a relatively clear and calm mind that is alert and ready to work. My best chance of reaching that ideal mindset is by observing *sīla*, so I do. When other students ask me for "tips" on maintaining their practice, my first answer is, "Observe *sīla*."

Often, however, people aren't eager to follow the precepts at home because they can feel like a too harsh and exacting list of rules. Having experienced the deep benefits of each one personally, I encourage you to try looking at them in a different light if that's the case for you. Instead of looking at the precepts as imposing on your freedom, look at them as a way to free your mind from negative habits that cause you unhappiness.

Take yourself back to primary school for a moment and you might recall a lot of rules. Classroom teachers need to find a way to encourage their students to follow these rules, and one of the strategies we use for creating student buy-in is to frame each rule in positive terms. For example, instead of stating "no hitting or no talking out of turn" we might say "in this classroom we are safe and respectful." This sets a different tone: the teacher isn't out to crush the students' freedom. Instead, they are shaping behavior in a way which creates a peaceful environment where students can focus on learning without being constantly anxious about their safety or having the opportunity to be heard without competition.

With the inspiring goal of freeing yourself from negative habits, it then becomes a joy to voluntarily undertake the training outlined in the precepts as a means of becoming more peaceful, compassionate, and happy.

1. Abstain from killing any being

In our house, we observe this precept by not killing insects or other animals that may enter. The children, too, have learned not to kill. We catch flies, for example, by capturing them with a cup against a window, sliding a stiff paper between the window and the cup, and then taking the fly outside to release it. Other critters can be handled similarly. I removed a non-venomous snake by covering it with a towel and grabbing the towel with tongs and releasing it outside. My partner and I also observe this precept by not hunting or fishing or eating meat, though the latter point is a matter of our own choice and interpretation of the precept. At this time, we still do prepare meat for our children because they were raised eating it and are not prepared to give it up.

My personal experience killing animals in the past (roaches in the house or raising chickens for food or fishing) is that along with the animal, I also suffered by killing them. I experienced so much heat, so much disturbance in my mind. How could I meditate with such an agitated mind? By choosing not to kill, my mind is so much calmer now, and I've even noticed my fear of insects has gone away.

2. Abstain from stealing

The literal Pāli-to-English translation of this precept is to abstain from taking what is not given, which to me, is much subtler than 'not stealing', as it is often presented in English. Either way, subtle or gross, this precept goes hand in hand with giving in to our greed and craving. And if we are giving in to craving in such an obvious way as taking something that doesn't belong to us, we are not well prepared to practice. The other motivation for stealing could be hatred if our aim is to take an object from someone to hurt them, whether or not the object has any importance to us. No matter the motivation, in neither case is the mind calm.

In an effort to fully observe this precept I've learned to restrain myself from taking things that are available but not specifically offered to me and to return things that I've held on to for ages but in fact were not my own—a violin from my university that I played for some twenty-five years being the most significant. Even though I ended up with it in my possession legitimately, in truth, it wasn't my own and had not been offered to me permanently. I feel better having notified the university and returned it (to a new and very surprised professor!). If you are adept at observing this precept in its gross form, see if you can also find ways to observe it more subtly.

3. Abstain from sexual misconduct

During courses and in monasteries, precept three is observed in a stricter version, which is to abstain from all sexual activity. Here, however, I will discuss only the version of the precept given to lay practitioners.

Sexual misconduct's definition can vary from culture to culture and generation to generation, but for our practical purposes, it means sex that is mentally or physically harmful to oneself or others. Sexual misconduct stems from greed and craving. Passion, like anger, can be difficult to overcome, but it is nothing other than an addictive flow of sensation, or *āsava*, as Goenkaji discusses in the Day 3 discourse of the 3-day course, that we can learn to be equanimous about and not react to. After suffering greatly from this addiction and experiencing the consequences, I am relieved to have peace in this area of my life now by having overcome the strength of passion through Vipassana.

4. Abstain from telling lies

This precept can also be translated as abstaining from wrong speech which includes abstention from malicious speech, harsh speech, gossip, and telling lies. The underlying wrong motivations here are hatred and greed. If I am hateful and greedy to the point that it is reflected in my speech, I am far from being able to concentrate my mind for meditation.

This precept, too, can be interpreted on very subtle levels, and we need to be patient with ourselves as we learn to recognize and ultimately change our ingrained habits of speech. For example, my partner was explaining the unfortunate situation for the workers in the hospital where my mother-in-law was receiving care, and while describing a worker's poor behavior, unpleasant sensations started coming up, and we realized we were breaking the precept by gossiping. At first, I tried to defend the conversation saying it was just an explanation, but afterwards I also felt it was unwholesome gossip and could have been left unsaid. By becoming more aware of our speech and acknowledging this kind of mistake, we have the opportunity to develop our *pāramīs* by generating loving-kindness and tolerance towards ourselves as we continue the work to use increasingly more wholesome speech.

5. Abstain from all intoxicants

There are two main reasons for abstaining from intoxicants. One is because they make us more likely to fail in observing the first four precepts. The second is because we lose our ability to maintain awareness. A very common motivation for taking intoxicants, even in arguably small amounts, is precisely to numb our awareness, either of pain or stress or both. In the practice, we seek to maintain awareness at all times, so taking intoxicants is moving in the exact opposite direction.

Subtlety here is again key to having ongoing success with this precept supporting our practice. Since all of us have completed at least one ten-day course, we know we can all go at least ten days without taking intoxicants, so a major hurdle has already been overcome. The biggest dangers left are in the occasional social drink and the grey area of a substance that may be taken for medication or recreation, such as cannabis. It's a slippery slope where our awareness starts to fail, our inhibitions and good intentions weaken, and we find ourselves breaking other precepts without ever having intended to.

Sīla, morality, is therefore paramount in establishing our practice because our minds become freed from new gross unwholesome actions and are made calm for practice. When we stop creating new *sankhāras*, the old ones, we are taught on Day 6, come to the surface, and, if we don't react to them, they pass away. Without maintaining *sīla*, we are constantly creating new unwholesome *sankhāras* and, even if we can overcome our agitation to practice, we won't have the opportunity to reach the deeper layers. It would be like sweeping with one hand while pouring sand on the floor with the other.

6

Pāramī

S*īla* is foundational to maintaining our practice and allowing progress, but it is only one in the list of ten mental perfections, called *pāramī*, that we must develop in ourselves in order to progress on the Path. On the organizational whiteboard in the Dhamma kitchen at the center where I frequently serve, the kitchen coordinator writes one *pāramī* at the top of the board each day to remind servers that we should be aware of developing those characteristics in ourselves during our service. At home, too, we should be ever aware of them. If your *sīla* is reasonably strong, but your meditation practice is still struggling, see which other *pāramī* could use more development. We all have room to improve.

The ten *pāramī*, or perfections, are

1. generosity (*dāna*)
2. morality (*sīla*)
3. renunciation (*nekkhamma*)

4. wisdom (*paññā*)
5. effort (*viriya*)
6. tolerance (*khanti*)
7. truth (*sacca*)
8. strong determination (*adhiṭṭhāna*)
9. selfless love (*mettā*)
10. equanimity (*upekkhā*)

In everything we do, there is the opportunity to increase our *pāramī*. The opportunity exists in the practice itself as well. So, in daily life, and in the practice, if we are aware of cultivating these characteristics in ourselves, we become engaged in a positive upward spiral where our behavior supports our practice, and our practice supports our behavior.

If you are reading this book because you have the intention to practice but are not in fact doing it, it is likely that you are judging yourself harshly for that too. A hard struggle for me and others I've talked with is not directing the benefit of these *pāramīs* towards ourselves. For example, I can be tolerant of other's failures but not my own. I can praise effort when I see it in a friend, but my own never seems to be enough. I can easily offer love to others but not to myself. At least I have become aware of this problem in myself so I want to point out that you may be doing it too. As you read the following paragraphs about the *pāramīs*, don't forget to consider how you treat yourself in regards to each one.

In Bhikkhu Bodhi's translation of *The Numerical Discourses of the Buddha*, it says "Bhikkhus, it is good for a bhikkhu from time to time to review his own failings. It is good for him from time to time to review the failings of others. It is good for him from time to time to review his own achievements. It is good for him from time to time to review the achievements of others." The *pāramīs* give us one way to reflect on our failings and achievements. What do we already have that we need to maintain, what do we lack that we need to increase? The answer will be different for each of us, but our goal, to attain them all, is common.

1. Generosity

Generosity opens our hearts and helps us understand that we are all equal: I am not more important; you are not separate from me. It helps break down our greed and ego and is a chance to share love with others in a tangible way. The foremost way my partner and I practice generosity is by giving regular financial support and service to our closest Vipassana center so others can also benefit from the practice. Of all the gifts I've ever received, the gift of Vipassana meditation has been the greatest, so as long as I'm able to give that gift to someone else, I will. A few other ways we practice generosity are volunteering at a homeless center and taking care of aging parents. However, the ways in which you practice generosity aren't the main point; it's your volition that counts.

Are you giving your time and money with love or out of a sense of obligation and with ill-will? Find a cause that genuinely touches your heart and start giving to that cause. Since you are an Old Student wanting to practice, serving at your Vipassana center might be a very good place to start!

2. Morality

As discussed earlier in the section on *sīla*, morality is the foundation of our practice. You experienced the benefit yourself during the ten days of your course. When our minds are agitated by killing, stealing, illicit sex, lies, and intoxicants, how can we be successful in meditation? Observing *sīla* calms our minds and readies us for meditative concentration. If you aren't observing the five *sīla* now, my suggestion is that you make it the first step towards establishing your practice. If you fail, simply acknowledge it and resolve again to keep the precepts.

3. Renunciation

By attending and serving courses, we experience a taste of what renunciation means and have the opportunity to develop this *pāramī*. After giving something up, we can look at it from a new perspective when the course ends. During a course, we renounce a lot of things: family, food preferences, entertainment, sleep, work, speech, exercise, etc. In daily life, we are spoiled without even realizing it.

One student was ecstatic to have freedom of speech again after coming out of a course, a "luxury" she'd never noticed before. Whenever I finish a course and return to life as usual, I find that many things I was attached to beforehand, whether they be material possessions or daily routines, weren't actually making me happier, they were only adding to the burdens I carry.

4. Wisdom

The wisdom of experiencing reality as it is and not as we want it to be, comes in its own time. So how can we hope to increase something we can't control ourselves? The answer is by paving the way for it to enter. If we remain self-centered and agitated and our minds are chaotic, we wouldn't recognize wisdom even if it came. By calming and concentrating our minds through the observance of sīla, and *ānāpāna* meditation when necessary, we keep ourselves fit to practice Vipassana. Practicing Vipassana, we learn to be aware of impermanence (*anicca*), suffering (*dukkha*), and no-self (*anattā*) and train ourselves not to blindly react to our sensations, thereby developing wisdom. So, prepare yourself and be watchful. This is why we practice.

5. Effort

Viriya is also sometimes translated as 'energy'. Like *sīla*, *viriya* seems foundational to me. If we don't muster our energy and make effort, we can't hope to succeed in meditation. It also takes effort to observe *sīla*. It's much easier to drink a glass of wine, relax, and fall into a comfortable bed than to sit on a mat, face my stress, and observe myself for an hour.

It also takes considerable effort to meditate outside of a course because external circumstances are often less than ideal. The house might be noisy with conversation, a TV might be on somewhere, music might be playing outside, someone is playing ball in the street, cars are zooming by under the window. We have to learn to tune in to ourselves instead of out to all the distractions. This is a great opportunity to increase our *viriya*!

6. Tolerance

In my culture, we are taught tolerance. Be tolerant of people with different beliefs and values, and habits. But often that "tolerance" comes with a heaping side of barely concealed ill-will. True tolerance comes with understanding and love. *Khanti* is also translated as patience. *Khanti* towards ourselves, *khanti* towards others, and *khanti* towards our circumstances all need to be developed.

Many students share the experience of spending a course sitting near another student who snores or passes gas or burps or has some other annoying habit during group meditation. For a couple of days, their agitation builds, and then, typically, they gain some insight that breaks that thought pattern and replaces it with *khanti*. For example, one young student was sitting by an older woman wearing many layers of silk clothing. Each time the woman moved, which was often, her neighbor could hear the cloth rubbing together. She became very agitated that this woman was so ignorant to wear such noisy clothes and move so often. But eventually, she realized that this woman was very old, was probably suffering a lot trying to maintain her posture during the hour sit and had probably always worn this type of clothing. None of it was intentional, and on top of that, she was working very hard. The agitation turned to *khanti*, and the student said once her mindset changed, she no longer heard the rustle of the fabric.

Khanti towards our circumstances can develop when we are in some kind of hardship. It goes along with equanimity and renunciation for me. For example, my partner had to leave the country unexpectedly to take care of ailing parents. At first, we counted our days apart, then weeks, then months. In total we counted five years. What choice do we have but to accept the reality as it is and not as we would like it to be? To do otherwise would only increase our suffering. *Khanti*, acceptance with a balanced mind, and letting go are our keys to continued peace and contentment in hard times.

Khanti towards ourselves is perhaps the hardest of the three to develop. I have a fair amount of tolerance for others, and I accept that I can't control all of my circumstances, but I like to think I can control myself. It can be frustrating when I realize I'm failing. Have you ever been the annoying student on the course?! The one who has to leave for the toilet ten minutes after the sit starts, the one whose stomach rumbles like thunder, the one wearing the noisy jacket, the one who drops the serving spoon or breaks a dish in the dining hall? Or at home do you have habits that remind you of things your parents did and cause you to feel frustration with yourself? Or you may have some other habits you've yet to overcome and you beat yourself up for them. *Khanti* is the medicine for that. I try to look at myself and smile as if I'm a child still learning because, on the Path, that's exactly what I am. Imagine you're watching a toddler learning to walk. You might say, "Oh, look how precious, struggling so much, surely success will come!" Goenkaji and our other teachers assure us success will come indeed. So, let's be patient with ourselves.

7. Truth

The *pāramī* of truth has enormous breadth and depth, but our focus here is truth in speech, as we observe in the fourth precept. As a child, I was taught to tell the truth, but quickly learned that truth didn't always get me what I wanted! Even then, I could feel the knots I was tying in myself by lying, but I couldn't overcome my greed, as innocent as it might have been in childhood, like lying about having stolen a few of my father's coins to buy candy.

The more I practice, however, the more I understand the consequences of those knots, and I am ever more determined to avoid tying new ones.

"White" lies too are still lies and bind us up internally. Even when it appears there are no external consequences, I can feel that I harm myself by not speaking the truth.

I seek opportunities now to confess what I have covered up in the past, and I resolve to keep the precept going forward. Speaking truth combats greed and frees our minds from the tension we create by lying, leading us towards liberation.

8. Strong Determination

Strong determination is another foundational *pāramī*. Without strong determination we can't undertake to observe *sīla* or sit twice a day or make ourselves sit still when we meditate or start again after we've given up. That is one of our lessons during a course—to exercise and increase our determination by sitting for an hour without moving. Though we aren't expected to keep ourselves as still off course, it takes continued and perhaps increased determination to practice at home where our minds are more agitated, and external conditions are often less than favorable. But don't underestimate yourself; if you finished a course, you can most certainly succeed in daily practice. If you have a break in your practice, just start again. Starting again is also evidence of your strong determination.

Some students, like myself, can have an imbalance of determination sometimes. I feel it goes along with a lack of tolerance and love for myself and excessive ego. Yes, we need a strong determination to succeed, but we also need to be understanding that the practice is difficult. If we get angry and frustrated with ourselves for not meditating the way we want to, we reinforce those negativities. Goenkaji explains on Day 2 that learning meditation is like taming a wild elephant. If we get angry, it only gets wilder.

9. Selfless Love

Also called loving-kindness, *mettā* is what we practice at the end of the ten-day course and at the end of each of our daily sits. And hopefully, a lot more frequently than that!

Mettā, selfless love, is just that—love with no thought of self. Frequently, though, our love is conditional and based on greed. I love you because you make me feel a certain way or you do certain things for me, and because you also love me in return for giving you similar good feelings, there's a cycle that seems to benefit both of us and feels pleasant. We call it love and are satisfied for a while. But when the cycle breaks, when I no longer get what I want from you, or when you no longer get what you want from me, we say we are no longer in love with each other. We are unsatisfied, and the truth of suffering reveals itself. In fact, we were never actually loving each other.

Mettā, however, is given unconditionally and is free from greed. As we develop the other *pāramīs* and purify ourselves from greed and hatred and delusion, our hearts open, and *mettā* increases. *Mettā* is inside everyone, though covered by layers of muck. This is why Goenkaji warns us to check ourselves before practicing *mettā* to see if we are fit to do so at that time. Be patient with yourself and stay watchful for spontaneous moments of its expression. Maybe you've felt loving-kindness naturally towards a close sibling or a best friend, or maybe to an animal. Once you notice it, can you purposefully extend it towards another being? I notice *mettā* increasing the more I practice Vipassana, and the more I stay aware of it even while not meditating. Buddha instructs us to extend *mettā* to all beings in all directions. Don't forget to include yourself!

Be aware too that *mettā* can perhaps sometimes be misunderstood—in other words, *mettā* isn't always cozy. The practice of *mettā* isn't to put ourselves in danger of being hurt or manipulated or to ignore unwholesome behavior. The point is to maintain an intention of goodwill, to wish others release from suffering no matter the circumstances, no matter how ignorant they are, no matter their current state. To offer a glaring example, working inside a prison

I am sometimes tasked with finding transitional housing for people who are being released and would otherwise be homeless. One man was having an unusually hard time finding a place to go because he had been convicted of a particularly gruesome crime. This is not someone I would want to have as an overnight guest, but I did genuinely wish him a safe, stable place to live, and was eventually successful in finding him an appropriate placement. His gratitude was immediate and overwhelming, and he was soon released to a new start. So, *mettā* allows for both the feeling of goodwill and the need for separation. One translation of the Ahina Sutta ends with the phrase "May the beings depart." There are many people in my life like this man to one degree or another. I send them *mettā* and genuinely hope they find peace, but I also know I'd better keep my distance.

10. Equanimity

Mental balance, evenness, and steadiness are hallmarks of equanimity or *upekkhā*. It's the state of mind where action takes the place of reaction. It's the ability to observe what's happening without being overcome by an impulsive response. One way to start becoming more aware of equanimity in general is to observe the lack of it in others. It's not unusual to notice people losing the balance of their mind over something that seems insignificant like an incorrect drink order at the coffee shop, or a missing pair of sunglasses. Can you then recognize those same tendencies in yourself? Once you train yourself to handle the small things in a balanced way, try to apply more equanimity to larger and larger issues. Eventually, we come to realize that there is nothing worth losing our hard-earned mental balance over. Things are as they are, and equanimity allows us to observe them as if from a safe distance and then choose how to act from a place of balance.

7

The Importance of Friendship

In the Pāli Canon literature, the importance of good friendship on the Path is emphasized. However, in daily life, far from Vipassana courses, friends who understand our aim to practice can seem non-existent. It is often possible to connect with other determined students, perhaps on a Metta Day when you can talk, or by giving service and meeting other Old Students. Other ways to connect are by joining online groups, attending group sits in person, or reading books written by others who are friends to all on the Path. At the same time, we must guard ourselves against unwholesome friends who lead us away from the practice, which is already difficult enough because of our own defilements.

When we finish a course, *sīla*, *pāramīs* and the teaching in general are likely to be at the forefront of our minds. Once back in the outside world, though, we are quickly distracted, and our thoughts are overpowered by mundane pursuits again. How can we maintain focus? Where can we find support? My answer has been threefold: *pariyatti* (the study of Dhamma), group sits, and giving Dhamma service.

8

Pariyatti

Listed below are two websites I've explored that have extensive Dhamma reading selections. They host everything from scholarly articles to streaming discourses to sutta translations to e-book downloads. Reading and listening to Dhamma reminds me of what's truly important to spend my time on, reinforces my understanding of the power and importance of the technique, and increases my faith and determination to continue on the Path. Reading has also greatly expanded my knowledge of the theoretical aspects of Dhamma, which, for me, has been a big benefit.

vridhamma.org
pariyatti.org

Another wonderful source of *pariyatti* for Old Students is the Dhamma.org app. On the app, you can find recordings in numerous languages of group sittings and discourses from several courses.

It also has recordings of the 10-day course morning chantings and numerous other chants. All of these can help you focus and maintain a good atmosphere during home meditation. The discourse recordings also provide you with another opportunity to hear Goenkaji speak, which I appreciate, because often during courses I am exhausted and in pain by the time the discourses begin.

9

Group Sits

So far, I've talked about internal factors that influence our ability to establish a daily practice, but another key factor in helping me establish my practice was external. I've found that having other Old Students I could talk to and sit with was indispensable.

Group sits are usually small groups of local students who meet together on a periodic basis to practice. They are an excellent way to meet other serious students and find wholesome friendships. If you don't have a group sit in your area, you can apply to become a host yourself. Aside from a few guidelines to ensure the meeting appropriately represents the practice, the requirements for the space are minimal.

Our local group meets in our living room. We live in a small town far from any center, and the largest gathering we've hosted has been just six students, but the support we've gotten in our small group has been enormous. The group has yielded more consistent practice for all of us, very strong friendships, wholesome business associates, and increased Dhamma vibrations in the house. Sitting together brings an energetic strength that I'm not able to create on my own, and that support can be crucial, especially in the beginning of a solo practice. You can use the Dhamma.org app to search for a local group, find a virtual group sit, or contact your local center to apply to be a host yourself.

10

Service

Giving Dhamma service is an invaluable gift to yourself and to those you are serving. It will greatly benefit your practice and the students on the course. During service, you do all the things I'm encouraging you to do in this booklet and more—sit three hours a day, maintain *sīla*, increase your *pāramī*, connect with other Old Students, make friends on the Path, and practice together. It's like a ten-day retreat to teach you how to practice while maintaining mundane responsibilities such as cooking and cleaning and living in harmony with others. There really can be no better laboratory to help you learn to implement the practice better than the service side of the retreat where you originally learned the technique! If you haven't had an opportunity to serve a course yet, I urge you to make it a priority.

Giving Dhamma service is hard work, but in an atmosphere of love and compassion and goodwill. I've never felt a workplace like that in the outside world. When I serve, I find my capacity to work increases so much because the motivation and the atmosphere are so good. I am happy to wake early and help prepare breakfast, and I am equally as happy to be still working into the evening hours. There is also ample time to meditate, talk to the other servers, and interact with the assistant teachers. I've met my closest friends and made some of my biggest progress while serving courses.

There are many ways to serve. If you've never served at all, I'd suggest starting with serving a ten-day retreat. You'll get the experience of serving a complete course and have a longer period to reap the benefits of being in that atmosphere. If that's impossible, there are usually opportunities to serve part-time or on shorter courses (3-day or 1-day).

Another option—if you're in a place in life where it is possible for you to spend more time at a center— is called 'sit-serve', where you typically serve two courses and sit one. After that, longer service may be an option for you to stay at the center and serve long-term, usually with a mentor teacher, and perhaps in a specific capacity like maintenance or operations management.

Other ways to serve are by joining one of the committees that support your local center. There are committee opportunities for all strengths, from finance to the kitchen, from children's courses to construction and IT. Ask your local center how you can be of service.

11

Sitting Once a Year

My final thought on establishing a daily practice is to make sure you are sitting courses regularly and not practicing other techniques. Goenkaji advises us to sit at least once a year. I look at it as the difference between brushing your teeth and going to the dentist. Sometimes there's only so much we can handle at home by ourselves—we need an environment where we can do the deeper work, ask questions when necessary, and have the necessary tools at hand to support us. And just think of the great opportunity you'll be giving others to serve you!

12

Conclusion

In my experience it is beneficial to return time and again to the concepts that Goenkaji so precisely and lovingly explains to us in his discourses. My aim here was simply to outline them and share some practical ways I have implemented his instructions in my life. Whatever personal situations you are experiencing will be different from mine, but the concepts remain the same as the Dhamma is truly universal.

Metta to all beings! May you be happy and free!

Acknowledgements

It was only with the help and support from other dedicated meditators that this booklet has come to be. I offer my sincere appreciation to William Hart for his careful consideration of the content to ensure that I have not distorted or misrepresented the teaching. I'd also like to express my gratitude to my husband Kostyantyn for his living example of a tireless commitment to the practice and for his patient companionship on the Path. I want to acknowledge Denis Chistyakov for encouraging me to move ahead after the first draft and for helping to move the project forward. I also want to thank local group sit members Rusty Black, Cristina Sasso and Akeem Richards for the opportunities to meditate and talk together and Stephan Novak for editing the text. Next, I would like to acknowledge Bill Crecelius and Brihas Sarathy for their support of this particular project and Steve Hanlon for his keen editorial eye and patience, Patricia Healy and Deborah Coy for their compassionate guidance, and all of the ATs, servers and other Old Students who have made my courses and service possible and supported me in the Dhamma. Each has made an indispensable contribution. Finally, I thank our lineage of past teachers, all the way back to the Buddha, whose boundless compassion compelled them to share the Dhamma and allow it to spread.

ABOUT PARIYATTI

Pariyatti is dedicated to providing affordable access to authentic teachings of the Buddha about the Dhamma theory (*pariyatti*) and practice (*paṭipatti*) of Vipassana meditation. A 501(c)(3) non-profit charitable organization since 2002, Pariyatti is sustained by contributions from individuals who appreciate and want to share the incalculable value of the Dhamma teachings. We invite you to visit www.pariyatti.org to learn about our programs, services, and ways to support publishing and other undertakings.

Pariyatti Publishing Imprints

Vipassana Research Publications (focus on Vipassana as taught by S.N. Goenka in the tradition of Sayagyi U Ba Khin)

BPS Pariyatti Editions (selected titles from the Buddhist Publication Society, copublished by Pariyatti)

MPA Pariyatti Editions (selected titles from the Myanmar Pitaka Association, copublished by Pariyatti)

Pariyatti Digital Editions (audio and video titles, including discourses)

Pariyatti Press (classic titles returned to print and inspirational writing by contemporary authors)

Pariyatti enriches the world by
- disseminating the words of the Buddha,
- providing sustenance for the seeker's journey,
- illuminating the meditator's path.